Living with a Work in Progress

A Parents' Guide to Surviving Adolescence

by Carol Goldberg Freeman

Illustrations by Katie Sullivan

National Middle School Association
Columbus, Ohio

National Middle School Association
2600 Corporate Exchange Drive, Suite 370
Columbus, Ohio 43231
1-800-528-NMSA

NMSA

National Middle School Association is a non-profit organization devoted solely to improving the education and development of young adolescents—those between the ages of approximately 10-15. Membership is open to parents and citizens generally as well as to educators.

For information on NMSA and its many services call 1-800-528-NMSA or write our national headquarters, 2600 Corporate Exchange Drive, Suite 370, Columbus, OH 43231.

Printed in the United States of America.

NMSA stock number 1237.

Library of Congress Cataloging-in-Publication Data

Freeman, Carol Goldberg, date
    Living with a work in progress: a parents' guide to surviving
adolescence/by Carol Goldberg Freeman.
        p.   cm.
    ISBN 1-56090-113-6 (pbk.)
    1. Teenagers—Family relationships. 2. Child rearing.
3. Parent and teenager. 4. Adolescent psychology.
I. Title.
HQ796,F7636   1996
649' . 125—dc20   96-36304
                                   CIP

Table of Contents

With love and thanks to
Brian, Tamara, Bill, and Truffle who are always with me
to share the sorrows, create the joys, and make me laugh at those times
when nothing seems funny.

PROLOGUE
Our National Secret Weapon

*L*iving with a Work in Progress: A Parents' Guide to Surviving Adolescence is a collection of articles on everything from anorexia to telephones to stereotyping to rejection. As its author, I hope to offer a few practical suggestions, a hearty laugh, and a reminder that your kid is not the only one who eats the science experiment. The brevity of the articles assumes that two minutes and thirty seconds is, likely, the maximum amount of uninterrupted time in your day.

Why is it that as the word "adolescence" is uttered, adults from Santa Clara to Chattanooga start to twitch and grip the arms of their chairs as if they are about to undergo a root canal with a pick-ax? Why is it that adolescents are often considered our national secret weapon? This book is designed to alter your perspective and help you look forward to a period that will never be dull. Thus, this book is written in celebration of adolescence.

We need to celebrate this period of tremendous change. We need to help our children celebrate their adolescence. For those readers who hyperventilate when the Cheerios are put back in the pantry on the "Oodles of Noodles" shelf, embracing change may prove extremely challenging. In fact, there are only two things you can count on: nothing is predictable and everything constantly changes. Reassuring message, isn't it? So, when your kids announce that they are going to color their hair in alternating rows of purple, lime green, and glow-in-the-dark orange, you are faced with a dilemma. On the one hand, you could shout, "fine, but you're not leaving this house till you have more wrinkles than a dried prune and your teeth are in a jar!" or you could do what my cousin Irma did. Celebrate the moment. She spray painted some mop refills so she had enough for the entire family to wear. Then, the next night at dinner even the dog was wearing a mop on top of its head. And all Irma ever said to her son was, "pass the butter, Honey."

I'm not saying that you should skip around the house singing "Zippity-Do-Da" and waving to the bluebirds. But, perspective is everything. So celebrate their adolescence. If your kids are not mutilating themselves or tying the dog to their rollerblades, celebrate these moments. Enjoy the zaniness of it all. As you try to keep pace with the changes, keep in mind that you are living with a work in progress.

And, when you put this book down you may discover that your kids have been cutting holes in the $40 jeans so they can look "cool." Before you grab the jeans and shriek, "you want ripped jeans? I'll show you ripped!" remember they will wear them that way and in front of your friends. So, instead, I'd opt for telling them that the going rate is $10 a hole, and as soon as they pay you, they can have them back.

Carol Goldberg Freeman

Uncommon Traits:
Snits, Zits, and Flammable Hair

Welcome to a retreat from the stresses and demands of everyday life, yet complete with all the modern conveniences. Enjoy your own special world. Above all, complete privacy is assured. Sound like an ad for an exotic Caribbean island? A Rockresort, perhaps? Believe me, this is no day at Elizabeth Arden. This is your kid's bedroom—according to your kid, of course, not you.

This sanctuary, almost religious in their minds, describes the dungeon to which we firmly sent our kids in the good old days as a cooling off place until they were civilized enough to join the rest of the family. Remember?

Now they come home from school, dump their book-bags on the kitchen floor, grab a couple of double-stuffs, and they're off and running. Where? To their room. Why? To call the friends they just saw in school all day.

Everything they truly value is safely smooshed and push-pinned into their rooms. The ski jacket, the soccer ball, the telephone, the Michael Jordan poster, 365 pages of the 1993 Joke-of-the-Day Calendar, Irving the gerbil, and that's only what we can see at a quick, surreptitious peek. (Interestingly, note where they choose to leave the book-bag!)

This rite of passage is really quite a normal developmental stage. For a period varying anywhere from one to three years, adolescents will rarely exit their room except to go to the mall. It is important to try to be patient with their need for privacy even if you have just foolishly spent $20,000 remodeling the house so your children will have a place to go when friends come over. In a world that always seems to try to control their lives, from parents to teachers to schedules, their room is the one place in which kids feel as if they are in control. (Face it, they don't even have control over their own bodies which are changing so rapidly they become unrecognizable).

So, please don't be too quick to call in the National Guard even if you are convinced they are up there experimenting with radioactive substances or, worse, making their hair look like their heads are on backwards. Remember, WE are the parents and we can always inflict upon them the worst punishment they could ever imagine: one full hour of playing cards with the entire family.

. . . .

"…but we used to be so close. She would tell me everything!" wailed yet another casualty of the adolescent rebellion. The good news is that this mutant who is inhabiting your daughter's body is not a permanent replacement. The bad news is that this behavior is not only normal, but healthy.

Adolescent girls, struggling to discover who they are and who they are not, want to find their own unique identity—separate from that of their mothers. What better way to do that than a complete and utter rejection of their mothers from our too white sneakers to our unpierced tongues? Keep in mind that adolescence is not a time of moderation. Feelings tend to go from love to hate faster than you can shriek, "looks like your hamster outgrew that skirt and gave it to you!"

So, how do we survive this rejection?

- First, I propose a temporary daughter exchange which could conveniently and cost-effectively be included in the classifieds. You might want to try this general format or make up your own. "Looking to swap 1 daughter—brown eyes, black lipstick, nose ring, cordless phone implant. Likes rap, fries, & Geraldo. No tattoos, please."
- Getting her to talk to you will probably require the use of a hydraulic jack—and even that just gets the lips moving. When you know she's upset and crying behind closed doors, let her know you're there if she wants to talk. If she doesn't, respect her need for privacy and just put your arms around her. She needs your support and comfort more than she realizes, without feeling pressured to spill her guts in return.
- Do you really want her to aspire to be a deodorant ad? She is desperately looking to emulate another adult female, so help her find one that hasn't been air-brushed. If that person cannot be you right now, maybe her math teacher or the artist next door or the physician down the street can reach out to her.
- Short-term counseling for the two of you might ease you both over the hump and help you learn how to balance her need for privacy with your need for closeness. See if she'll

agree to go once and actually get out of the car before you threaten to send for the Jaws of Life. She needs to feel that she has some control over the plan.

Just don't jump out of your matched accessories if you scan the classifieds and find, "looking to swap one mother: brown eyes and nosy. Likes Oprah and caesar salads. Non-speaking only."

. . . .

And my kids complain because I don't talk to them the way I talk to my dog? It certainly couldn't have anything to do with the fact that Truffle doesn't ever argue with me, always puts her toys away, and never fights over the video games, could it? Wouldn't it be wonderful to simply shake your finger, sweetly say, "no, no, little one", and have our children skulk, wag their tails, and look contrite? Instead, we get "it's not fair" or "why is it always my fault?" or the "if looks could kill" pout.

Why is it that although our kids may have enthusiastically embraced setting the table for the last five years, they now find it violates their human rights? Why is it that they used to fight for the privilege of changing Truffle's water and now they whine that they did it the last three times and you make them do everything cause you want them to experience oppression firsthand?

They are adolescents—that's why. Face it, you could even say, "don't bother, dear. Let me do it for you," and they would challenge you.

You can try to minimize conflict by involving your children in setting the limits. With their participation in the process, you are more likely to enlist their cooperation. For example, kids are much more likely to wash their hair on a regular and frequent basis if they have, in advance, agreed that it is a reasonable demand in the first place. If not, don't be too surprised if their hair becomes a flammable substance before they feel a shampoo is necessary.

Setting clear, precise expectations might also avoid some potential battles. For example, "please take the kitchen garbage out on Monday and Thursday immediately following dinner" has a slight chance of actually working. It allows no room for interpretation. Go ahead and try saying, "it's your job to take out the garbage." Congratulations! You will soon be the proud owner of an indoor, seven foot high garbage dump, conveniently located right in your very own kitchen. And your children will, truly, not even notice it's there until it dares to enter their room without knocking.

However, while you may deftly stave off a confrontation or two with some practice, I still wouldn't advise you to light a match within two football fields of the hairdo.

. . . .

Remember when your kids used to save over half their "Happy Meal" hamburger? Things surely have changed! Now, your child's appetite more closely resembles an industrial vacuum cleaner. On the other hand, you may be living with the opposite extreme: your child may have decided that a balanced meal is half a string bean slowly chewed twenty times before swallowing. Unfortunately, the words "moderation" and "balanced" are not part of an adolescent's repertoire. When they are hungry they consume faster than a paper shredder. When they have decided they are too fat, they, simply, stop eating.

Adolescent girls are often at risk for eating disorders. Self-esteem is at the heart of this problem combined with a desire for more control over their lives. These girls may think that if they only get all A's or lose 15 pounds, they will feel better about themselves. However, these accomplishments do not help them feel better or happier. Instead, these girls keep trying to be the perfect student or lose just a few more pounds. Thus, it is with pride that they delve into their hearty meal of a carrot stick. Does this mean that your daughter, who is convinced she's fat and insists on wearing the to-the-knees tee shirt over everything, might have an eating disorder? Not necessarily. Practically every adolescent girl looks into the mirror at toothpick legs and sees two giant Redwoods staring back at her. Here are some signs to watch for:

- Frequent weighing.
- Refusal to eat and denial of hunger.
- Depression.
- Loss of or no onset of menstrual cycle.
- Lusterless, dry skin and hair.
- Preoccupation with food, calories.
- Significant weight loss.
- Excessive exercising.
- Irritability and withdrawal.

So, even if you are tempted to grab the milkshake, fries, and Devil Dogs your son was about to munch on just to hold him till dinner and inject it into your daughter, please don't. Instead, try the following:

- Talk openly with her about your concerns.
- Praise her for herself and not for her appearance or accomplishments.
- Get yourself some good, sound advice from a physician or psychologist whom you trust.

When your daughter sobs that if she lost some weight maybe Jamie would like her, it is not particularly constructive to shriek, "Jamie? That self-centered little slug who smooshes worms with his teeth!" You might calmly suggest taking her to a physician or a nutritionist for some advice (face it, she's more likely to listen to a five pound chicken than to you, anyhow). Then, tomorrow, put a stocking over your head, hide in the bushes at Jamie's bus stop and spray-paint the little twerp purple.

Friendship:
Susie Teitlebaum and Other Tales of Woe

"**I** HAVE NO FRIENDS" are the four little words that make us want to hang the little terrorists next door by their ankles and tickle their feet till they beg for mercy and swear they will be best friends with your child forever.

Your kid, in ten years, may not, necessarily, be destined to live alone in the Ozarks with a pet warthog and a bottle of moonshine. The "I have no friends" proclamation may really be translated in a variety of ways:

- Nobody saved me a seat at lunch today.
- It's Friday night and my best friend is going to the game with someone else.
- We have to work in groups in English and I'm not with any of my friends.

Although perspective is everything, it seems to have been removed, by laser beam, from every adolescent slouching around the globe. Instead, everything is a crisis. One pimple behind their hairline and, from now on, their only public appearance will be at the movie theater after the Jimmy Fund collection has been completed. One request to help with the dishes and they behave as if you've asked them to clean out the baboon cages at the Bronx Zoo.

So, how do you ground them in reality? If you think reason and logic will prevail, forget it. As soon as you say, "what kind of a thing is that to say! You have lots of friends. What about…?" they'll scream, "they all HATE me!" as they slam the door in your face.

In early adolescence, peer approval becomes paramount. As parents and teachers we can tell our children they're the best thing since nose rings, but until they see evidence of it from the other kids at school, it will mean nothing. Developmentally, these young adolescents are separating from adults. In order to do so, their identification shifts completely. In fact, to gain peer acceptance your well-mannered child may even be willing to push the limits of good taste. Reports to incredulous parents that their child distinguished him/herself by demonstrating the art of spit-balling during the chapter ten exam are not uncommon. Despite these dismal findings, here's what you can do:

- Acknowledge their feelings by saying, "You must feel horrible right now."
- Try to get them to tell you what makes them feel as if they have no friends.
- When you know more about the specific situation, you can say something like, "it sounds as if you're really hurt that…"

Now, you can begin, the two of you, to deal constructively with the actual situation at hand. More than likely, within the next twenty minutes you will have eagerly baked a chocolate cake and canceled your anniversary weekend in the Poconos to stay home and go to "Bowl O Mart" with your child. As you suggest that you both get going and he/she says, "I'd love to, really, but Jamie just invited me to sleep over. You don't mind, do you?" remember, perspective is everything.

. . . .

Phew! You've made it through eight weeks of summer togetherness. Eight weeks of putting up with the kids down the street who polish off your three pound bag of tortilla chips in one sitting, who plunk down their bikes in your driveway just when you come roaring up and, who have, to all appearances, moved in until they collect their first social security check. At least now that school has started, we can focus our children on more intellectually and culturally suitable friendships—or can we?

We may fantasize about our children forming deep and meaningful relationships with their peers based on mutual respect, trust, and 8:00 curfews. But the reality is otherwise. Teen-agers seem magnetically attracted to the kid with the glow-in-the-dark hair or the kid who can lasso the bus driver.

We can intercede only in sly and subtle ways. Why not kill them with kindness by insisting that they invite the little subversive over to your house? That gives you some control over what is going on. But more than that, the invitation will probably never be issued. How appealing would it be for your kid to launch ink balls from his/her own family room? That sort of activity is best done wherever the parent is not.

As tempting as it might be to lash out and say, "this kid's a bozo, and will only be asked over when I lock myself out of the house and need an expert to break in," I have found it more effective to let my children know what I think of their taste in friends but to stop short of forbidding the friendships. For example, I might say, "look, anyone who actually eats the science experiment sounds weird to me. But if you think it's cool, the kid's certainly welcome to come over."

What it means is high visibility for us, high accountability for the kid. So, you need to be there. Look, somebody's got to take a head count of the goldfish before the kid goes home, right?

· · · · · · · · · ·

Susie Teitlebaum. It really didn't even matter that she didn't invite me to her boy/girl party in seventh grade cause I knew it was going to be boring and dumb. The boys would put potato sticks up their noses, throw pizza bombs, and make disgusting noises and the girls would all stand together, giggling about the boys. I was relieved, yes, relieved, and grateful that she never had the common decency to include me on her guest list. My mother told me it was "just a party" and, besides, Susie Teitlebaum was probably jealous of me (Susie with her long chestnut hair and prematurely voluptuous body).

As these inevitable rejections happen to our own children maybe we can offer a little more understanding than our parents gave to us. My mother couldn't do much about Susie Teitlebaum's party, but she could have acknowledged my complete and utter misery at the time. A simple "you must feel really hurt" and a hug would have been appreciated. She needed to understand that she could never convince me I wasn't a freckle-faced toad and any attempts to do so were about as believable as Susie Teitlebaum stuffing 25 watt light bulbs into her bra. Making sure that I was busy the night of the party, would have helped, too. But, as sure as I tragically pined for a week like a Bette Davis heroine, if my mother had told me to invite some friends to sleep over I'd have shrieked, "All my friends are going to the party. The only kids who aren't are LOSERS!" Nowadays, malls and video rentals can provide the diversion.

Think of these experiences as character building. We all have Susie Teitlebaums in our past. From these rejections we begin to learn who we are and who we aren't. We learn who our friends are and who they aren't. In time, of course, we mature and mellow. Why, in the almost thirty years since Susie Teitlebaum's party, it is obvious that I've practically forgotten the entire, ugly, destructive, vicious, hurtful incident! I often think kindly of

Susie Teitlebaum. In fact, I often think of her as I truly hope she is today: gray hair and balding, fifteen extra pounds slapped onto each thigh, and warts all over her nose.

. . . .

"Mom, by the way, Terry invited me to sleep over Friday night, okay?" Terry? TERRY? Either the extra large bag of cheese doodles you inhaled at lunch induced amnesia or this combination of sounds has never been pronounced by your child. You fight the impulse to say, "Sure, I'm bringing my sleeping bag along, too" and, instead, calmly inquire about the proposed host. The story usually has one of two endings: either you incur the wrath of your children by refusing to let them go or you spend Friday night in constant fear that they are cruising the Interstate on the back of a motorcycle.

What do we do when our children begin to establish friendships with kids who could have just stink-bombed the middle school, for all we know? Prior to these years, our children's friends were often children in the neighborhood or children of our own friends. The peace of mind we had when our children went off to play with the friends we had chosen for them is threatened now. Their social explorations can cause us to start twitching every time the phone rings. The good news is that this independence is healthy and very normal. The bad news is that, according to our kids, any concern on our part classifies us as federal undercover agents. Well, the bad news for them is that I'd have to be threatened with having to let my roots grow out before even thinking about backing off. The secret is vigilance, not control: be involved but not overprotective.

• Since you don't know Terry you could encourage your child to invite him/her to your house, first. You might ask the parents to come in for a few minutes when they drop Terry off.

• You might tell your child that you will be calling Terry's parents to check out the what the plans are and who will be present before making a decision.

• On the night of the sleepover, it is perfectly appropriate, and advisable, for you to walk inside with your child, not necessarily to case the house for signs of a mentally competent adult, but to help carry the sleeping bag, of course.

• Your new career as "chauffeur" provides a marvelous opportunity to work under cover. Kids really believe that because the driver stares silently straight ahead, it is physically impossible to hear the remarks blasted into your eardrums from the back seat. Thus, you quickly will be able to determine which kids you feel uneasy about. Subtlety is not part of an adolescent's repertoire.

And, don't worry—with any luck the first sleepover could be at your house!

. . . .

Why am I so fascinated with Woodstock (the real Woodstock of 25 years ago, of course)? It's for the same reason that I dyed my gym suit shocking pink and then refused to wash it my entire ninth grade year. It's for the same reason I wore dirndl skirts and wanted to have Rosary Beads and went out with Bucky Martin. I wanted to belong.

I wanted to experience Woodstock. I wanted to have mud oozing from between my teeth. I wanted to sing *With a Little Help from My Friends* and tell people my name is Moonbeam. I wanted to share a tent with a bearded pony-tailed revolutionary. But I didn't. My parents would have killed me!

Is this very different from your kids asking to be picked up after the movie at 11:30 even though it ends at 9:05? Do you think they actually LIKE standing on the corner trying to look cool and hide their cigarettes when your friends drive by? Of course not. They want to belong.

This gathering is their Woodstock, and you have the right to NOT allow it. Here's the secret: do what your kids do—unite and try the collaborative approach. Even the Three Stooges didn't do it alone. So, what makes us think that we can conquer adolescence single-handedly? But, as a unified force, maybe we have a chance. Call some of their movie friends' parents and say, "it seems that our kids want to hang out on the corner in the dark for two hours. I'm sure it's not ecologically desirable and I'm not comfortable with it, are you?" Perhaps, you can all agree to give them an extra twenty minutes to get pizza or ice cream instead.

Look, establishing a parent-communication hotline can only make our job easier. If we can convince our kids that the Internet automatically transmits their whereabouts to every parent on the Eastern seaboard, think of the power this gives us!

Despite my longing to belong, I do find some comfort in knowing that I didn't make the cover of *Newsweek's* "Woodstock Retrospective." We can all celebrate the spirit of Woodstock—without exposing every freckle to the world.

. . . .

Do you remember how it felt when your very best friend got the lead in the school play and you were a purple crocus? Do you remember how hard it was to congratulate the best friend who made the cheerleading squad when you didn't? I remember my best friend when I was thirteen years old. She was a wonderful friend—bright, pretty, thoughtful, funny, popular. Most of the time I adored her, but at times I became insanely jealous of her and would have loved for her to walk to the blackboard with a wedgie. The normal insecurities of adolescence were only heightened when I compared myself to someone whom I believed was perfect. We're always going to find someone who is brighter, prettier, funnier, more popular, more athletic, more artistic. Helping our children appreciate who they are, unique in all the world, is our challenge as parents. Jealousy is a fact of life. How we learn to cope with it is important.

How do you help your children to confront and get past the jealousy?

- If you can get them to acknowledge this emotion that's a good start. Maybe they can tell you or their friend that they get very jealous at times. Sometimes a journal can be a comfortable way to express feelings if saying them aloud is difficult.
- Next, you need to acknowledge the jealousy rather than give the expected "good mother" speech—"Oh, Honey, you're even prettier and smarter than Lisa." Let them know that it hurts to feel jealous, but that it's perfectly normal.
- Then, try talking to them about ways in which they are alike as well as ways in which they are different from their friend. Who cares that their best friend got the lead in the play since they prefer spending their time on the soccer field rather than the stage anyway.
- Finally, it wouldn't be a bad idea to delicately disclose a jealousy of your own and how you've coped with it. It would reassure your kids that jealousy is a part of life if they knew that you had felt it from time to time yourself.

My own opportunity presented itself sooner than I could have hoped. Last week my mother called and told me all about driving four hours each way to dog-sit, once again, for my sister's pug, Buster, who kept hitting the electric window button, got his tongue caught in the window, and had to live on Italian ices for the next two weeks. "Humph! Would she have inconvenienced herself like that to dog-sit for MY dog?" I brooded. I hung up, ate half a box of chocolate Pinwheels, and screeched, "See, I could care less that my mother still loves my sister more than me!"

With age comes wisdom; with wisdom comes serenity.

. . . .

"Rose, it must be telephonitis!" I gasped then calmly read, "telephonitis: a chronic condition in which first signs often appear in early adolescence. While a cure is not yet available, treatment can be effective if begun at onset of symptoms with frequent monitoring."

One case study involves the kid who becomes mute when grandma calls up from Peoria, but shows signs of verbal nausea when unidentifiable friends merely breathe at the other end of the line. The same kid whose idea of an articulate response is "yeah" as the eyeballs roll across the top of their sockets is now perversely attached to a device completely dependent on verbal communication. While you are probably pleased by this developmental milestone, you probably also share my horror of chronic telephonitis.

This epidemic, sweeping the adolescent population, is actually a very important part of the socialization process. When I was growing up I could easily walk or ride my bike to my friends' houses after school. We all could meet in the park whenever we wanted to get together. However, today, parents often have to drive kids from friend to friend. Informal gatherings don't occur so easily. The only independent form of socializing that can take place outside of school is on the phone. Do you realize that what we call "wasting time on the phone" is our kids learning to listen, expressing their feelings, resolving conflicts, deciding whether to wear your blue sweater to school tomorrow? And they have even learned the art of the conference call. In fact, their proficiency has greatly surpassed us .

Although my ultimate goal is to be able to talk to my mother on the phone and balance the checkbook at the same time, I find it challenging just trying to eat bagel chips without my friend, at the other end, hearing the tell-tale crunch. Our kids, though, can simultaneously juggle two friends on the line, "General Hospital," and pre-algebra with amazing aplomb.

However proud we may be of our children's telephonic techniques, we need to keep this device available to the entire family. So, here are a few practical suggestions:
• Privacy is an essential ingredient for a good, long conversation. Locate phones in the

family room and/or kitchen and install a cord no longer than a rubber band.

- Worse than having to identify themselves is the agony of conversing with an adult. So, engage every little caller in a lengthy conversation and that's the last you'll hear of them.
- While "call waiting" may, indeed, be the rudest invention since plunking down twenty-five items on the twelve item lane, it, at least, enables us to maintain contact with the outside world.
- Scheduling phone time can work, provided your children understand that either they inform their friends or you will.
- Time limits tend to be very ineffective. They hang up from one call and, simply, start the meter all over again.

My neighbor, Rose, had a plan to treat telephonitis: her kids had to pay 10¢ a minute and leave the money in the empty coffee can on the kitchen counter. Rose figured that she'd either brilliantly control this outbreak or have enough money at the end of six months for a day at the Norwich Spa, complete with mud bath. After three months, however, there were no visible signs of progress. Rose's mother from Peoria had feigned one stroke, two dognappings, and one hostage attempt to get the operator to break through the busy signal, and the kids were still fighting over the phone. Dreaming of massages, New Age music, and herbal tea, Rose greedily ripped off the lid to find the can empty except for a note stuffed in the bottom: "Mom, the 10¢ a minute idea is great . I figure that by talking on the phone I actually saved you 64 trips driving me to my friends. So, I just deducted 10¢ a mile. I figure that you owe me only about $17.50. A bargain, really!! Love, Allie."

Schoolwork:
Choosing Your Battles

"So, what did you get on your math test?" middle school parents from Monterey to Tuscaloosa are asking as they pass the ketchup. While mastering the content of the curriculum is important, demonstrating a minimal level of respect should be of equal importance. Imagine how smugly satisfying it would be to growl, "Toby, you got an A in science for your 'Talking Termites' project. Congratulations! But, what have we here—an F in RESPECT for taking Jesse's Ring Ding and smooshing it with your elbow?"

The school community is the "real world" for your adolescent. These are the years in which they learn how to interact with the world around them. At times they will lie, cheat, bully, and make you want to volunteer them to test bungee cords. However, keep in mind that they are a work in progress and may be super-gluing their tongue to their locker one day and organizing a recycling effort the next. Therefore, we must view their indiscretions as opportunities for growth. But, we must make it absolutely clear that we place a high value on respect and be prepared to stand by this priority. Without respect for self, others, and the environment, your child is like a moose with a stomach bug—a creature nobody particularly enjoys having around.

As parents, then, how do we let our kids know that respect in school means more than not getting caught? How do we let our kids know that the way they treat their world may have more value than reciting every state capital? How do we let our kids know that we prefer baboon breath to rude and obnoxious?

Maybe tonight we need to ask them a slightly different set of questions.
• What did you do today that was helpful to someone?
• Who did something to help you today?

Maybe we should try responding to these questions ourselves. In this way, we let our children know that these values are relevant to our life, too.

And, maybe it wouldn't be such a bad idea to grade RESPECT just as we do science, English, and math. It might make a difference when we glance at our kid's report cards and say, "Hmmm. Looks as if you didn't make the honor roll: an F in RESPECT."

. . . .

"Tell me. How was your first day back?" my husband asked cheerily.

"Fine!" I barked, slamming my book bag against the wall as I stomped to the kitchen and stuffed three Twinkies into my mouth at once.

"Was it fun to see everyone?" Bill continued, ignoring my snit.

"Sure," I snapped back spitting Twinkie filling halfway across the room. Couldn't someone manage to empty the dehumidifier or are they planning to use the water to cook the spaghetti?

"It must have been fun not having the students around yet."

"Yeah," I smiled politely. (It was also *fun* to sit around all day at work ruminating over whether the smell of half-empty glasses of milk on the kitchen counter would make me pass out or vomit when I got home).

I really love work. However, adjusting to the routine and the pace is a change I resist heartily. During the summer the dirty laundry could be doing a Conga line through the living room and I'd simply join in. But after September 1, I'm likely to take a blow-torch to the person who puts an empty Ben and Jerry's container back in the freezer.

Why is it, then, that we expect our kids to abruptly switch to Budapest Standard Time, eat lunch in twelve and one half minutes, wear shoes, and do homework before dinner, AND tell us all about it as soon as they walk through the door? Why is it we are convinced their teachers eat pick-up trucks for breakfast or that our kids are latent sociopaths if they don't seem to enjoy school right away? Just the separation anxiety of having to leave the Yankees hat at home is enough to produce traumatic stress syndrome.

They may need a month or so to ease into school. You can help by sensing when they don't want to talk and respecting that wish. It is certainly important that they start out with good study habits, etc., but help them also find opportunities to stare at their zits and be thoroughly non-productive.

Of course, being a school psychologist makes me more aware of these subtleties than most parents. So when my son walked in the door yesterday I said cheerily, "Tell me. How was your first day back?"

"Fine," he barked, slamming his book bag against the wall as he stomped to the kitchen and reached for the empty package of Twinkies that I had put back in the pantry.

. . . .

All right, so the first report card was not quite what you had expected. So, there won't be a Nobel Prize winner in the family this year. Okay, maybe it's really true, just as your kid said. They've changed the marking system this term—reversed the letter order. Well, let's face it: the report card stunk. Still, is that any reason to wear black and go into mourning for the demise of your child's intellect? It may be somewhat early to assume that your heir-apparent is headed for a future mucking out elephant cages.

This is what middle school is all about. It is a period of tremendous ups and downs as your child goes through various stages from free spirit to sophisticate to slug. Fortunately, these stages never last. They seem to be constantly replaced by a new and unprecedented phase. The boy with the crew cut who sat across from me in seventh grade earth science turning his eyelids inside out, is now an eminent ophthamologist. Who would have guessed?

What can we do, then, besides grounding our kid for life?

- We need to be involved on a day-to-day basis in helping our children set short-term, realistic goals. Expecting our kids to remember when to use commas may not be reasonable when they can't even remember what shirt they're wearing. But, expecting our kids to work for thirty minutes on their rough draft, go back and circle all the words they aren't sure they spelled correctly may be perfectly reasonable.
- Banishing our kids to their rooms to work in a quiet place may prove to be as productive as our trying to work on income taxes on a beach in Tahiti. More than likely, your kid will become quite adept at lying on the floor of the bedroom, carefully wadding up scraps of perforated-edged, two subject notebook paper into balls which are pitched at the ceiling and land in the wastebasket. Instead, the kitchen or dining room table might be better suited for study time.
- Letting your kids know that you are in frequent communication with their teachers

goes a long way towards encouraging accountability. What fun would there be in burping out the "Star-Spangled Banner" if they thought their parents would be immediately notified of this remarkable accomplishment?

• Lastly, it is important to try to be supportive, not punitive. Although it's tempting to threaten you child with hanging a "Room for Rent" sign in his/her window, this approach may not be constructive. When the disappointing test grade arrives, praise your child, at least, for spelling his/her name correctly. Then ask what he/she might do *differently*, not *better*, next time.

Helping your child feel competent and experience success is the best way to assure future successes in school. Come on, middle school may be the best five years of your kid's life.

. . . .

The books and coat are angrily hurled across the kitchen as your child stomps upstairs, slamming the door, and all you said was, "Hi, Honey. How was school today?" There just may be a subtle message in this: *stress*.

Of course, as adults we are in much better control and never resort to such flights of immaturity. I recall a few weeks ago the morning we were all doing our usual rushing around to our precision schedule when my daughter, Tam, shrieked as she let the dog inside. At 6:45 A.M. Eastern Standard Time Truffle was sprayed in the face by an irate skunk. Attempting to remain calm in a crisis and model effective coping skills, I remembered that tomato juice removes the odor. Naturally, I was out of tomato juice. Thus, Truffle was whisked into the tub and bathed in Prego Spaghetti Sauce with mushrooms, instead. It didn't work. I was late, smelled like "l'essence de skunk," and was rather unpleasant to be around in every sense of the word.

We certainly know the signs when we are about to go over the edge. How can you know when your child is under stress? Noticeable changes in eating or sleeping patterns might be symptoms of stress. Recent lethargy, drop in grades, difficulty getting along with friends and family are other possible signals to you that your child needs your help and understanding to better cope with stress at this time.

So, what do you do about it? You can start by asking them if they're feeling pressured lately. They'll probably be so surprised that they're not being reprimanded for losing their temper that you might even shock them into telling you what is bothering them. Who knows? If this doesn't work don't assume they need intensive psychotherapy because you never played Mozart string quartets to them in utero. Start with the simpler assumptions first. Maybe they feel there is too much to do in a given day.

- Rather than becoming Attila the Hun and insisting they begin to do homework for three hours before dinner, you might want to consider a gentler approach. "You seem to have a lot of work to do tonight, so I'll be glad to clear the table for you," would go a long way to showing that you understand their stress and are willing to pitch in and help. Maybe they'll even return the favor when you need them to.

- Offering to sit down and help your child organize his/her time before he/she gets frantic might avoid potential explosions. The trick, of course, is to catch your kid before the panic sets in.

- Suggesting a walk or a half hour errand with you as a study break might be a welcomed relief. Even taking out the garbage has been known to sound appealing to kids stuck in the middle of a report on the U.S. Constitution. Actually, here's your chance to get their bedroom cleaned up, Anything sounds better than that report.

- If the symptoms persist more than a few weeks, you should check out your concerns with the pediatrician. Input from your child's teachers would be a help at this point.

By the way, a stressful experience can be a learning experience for everyone. I learned that a remedy better than tomato juice is found among the feminine hygiene products. Think of the possibilities!

Boyfriends & Girlfriends:
Life on the Richter Scale

I waited in the car while my little boy went to the door to pick up his little friend for the seventh grade "get-together." The entire way in the car, he and his best friend Josh had been in the back seat shoving and wrestling like a couple of puppies. Then, Brian exited and returned with someone who looked like she must have been his older sister and wearing a dress that could fit into a plastic sandwich baggie.

"Mom, this is Courtney."

"Oh, are you the same Courtney who has been calling Brian for seventeen days straight and giggling when I answer the phone? Are you the same Courtney who has been identifying herself as "Melissa, Beth, and Jessica" whenever I ask who it is? Are you the same Courtney who has even managed to keep Spike the iguana from getting a full night's sleep with your late phone calls?" I wanted to screech in her six-holed pierced ear. But, instead, I politely replied, " Very nice to meet you. Aren't you going to FREEZE like that?"

The week after the "get-together" was consumed with phone calls at an accelerating rate, answering machine messages telling my son he is "Hot Stuff" and shocking pink envelopes with hearts, doused with the 90's version of "Ambush." At the same time, Brian began to find a myriad of excuses to be out of the house. I began to benefit from his desire to escape and found that the garbage was taken out without my asking, Truffle our dog was walked frequently, and for the first time in years we didn't find a note in our mailbox from our neighbor, "MOW YOUR DAMN LAWN! MY PEONIES CAN'T GET ANY SUN."

Brian seemed unusually volatile and moody lately, but it was the phone call during sloppy joes on pumpernickel that brought on the explosion. "Well, Hot Stuff, it's for you, again," his sister sneered, lips not moving, eyebrows flipping out of her forehead. With that, Brian threw down his fork, dropping sloppy joe onto Truffle's incredulous snoot, and stormed up to his room crying.

After arguing about which one of us would pick up the phone and tell Courtney that Brian wasn't available, I went upstairs, knocked on his door and was, reluctantly, granted admittance. "I hate her!" he sobbed.

"Sweetie, I know your sister shouldn't have teased you, but…"

"It's Courtney I hate! She keeps bugging me and won't leave me alone. She leaves notes in my locker, follows me to class. I can't get away from her!" he wailed, his voice hitting high C.

With this revelation, I thought of how desperately Brian had tried to become invisible lately, hoping to avoid this thirteen year old predator. The range in maturity and sophistication, particularly between boys and girls, is never greater than during adolescence. While Courtney is fantasizing about romance, Brian's fantasies probably include a ball and baseball bat. So I helped him compose a brief "I just like you as a friend" letter; and, until that directed her hormones elsewhere, I was fully prepared to intercept the phone calls.

Of course, the opportunity arose within the next ten minutes. When the phone rang and Brian did a jackknife under his blanket, I picked up and assumed my mother's commanding tone, capable of reducing telemarketing salespeople to blubbering.

Look, I had to do something. You can't imagine what it's like to live with an iguana suffering from sleep deprivation.

. . . .

Your daughter's in love! Isn't that wonderful? He's cute and he's cool. What else matters—to her, that is? To you, it means that she has established permanent residency in front of the bathroom mirror practicing her smile and the rest of the family would find it easier to gain access to box seats at the World Series. To her, it means that she is accepted and validated. To you, it means that she is as preoccupied as a male with the remote control box and has painstakingly begun ironing her shirts, remembering to return the iron to the refrigerator where it belongs. To her, it means that she is "hot."

But what happens when, two days later, he is in love with another hot thirteen year old—probably one of her good friends? Will she shave her head and run, screaming, through the streets? Will she throw herself into the microwave without first remembering to remove yesterday's Spaghettios? How can a parent help a daughter through these traumas?

With nostalgic bitterness, I remember one of my first boyfriends. Miraculously, we were an item for sixty-seven hours, fourteen minutes. The excitement of walking down the hall with him was contrasted with the terror I felt as I could think of nothing whatsoever to say to him. It was amazing that once officially categorized as boyfriend, Ira Rosenberg, who had thrown spitballs at me since third grade, now seemed as foreign as the spit curls that popped straight out like antennae, refusing to adhere to my cheeks.

Okay, so it's now two days later and the inevitable has occurred: he dumped your daughter. You know by being alert to subtle signs such as her slamming the back door so hard the jar of poultry seasoning you were looking for last week jumped off the shelf and crashed to the floor. Warning: DO NOT be solicitous. You'll live to regret it. If you say, "Honey, what's wrong?" she will shout, "NOTHING!" so loudly it will cause a tidal wave in your toilet bowl. Instead, you might quietly ask her to help you clean up the broken glass. Wait a few hours before attempting a conversation.

When she is ready to let loose and talk, you may find, as my mother did, what being in love with Ira Rosenberg was really all about. Through my convulsive sobbing and hysteria, I screeched the humiliating, unspeakable truth. I didn't even LIKE Ira Rosenberg, but he dumped me before I could dump him. Vanity, thy name is Teenager.

. . . .

Did you happen to catch the solo synchronized swimming event in the Olympics? "Solo" synchronized swimming? Come on! The commentator goes wild as a big toe rises from the water, looking like a periscope spying on the enemy. You've got to be kidding! My eight year old did that in the pool yesterday while I was reading about summer camps for mothers—the part about being tucked in and read to by a Tom Cruise look-alike, so I hardly even glanced up.

Solo synchronized swimming is truly a metaphor for life: how easy it would be if we lived in isolation. My kids wouldn't make fun of me when I try to convince them that going to garage sales is a "family bonding" experience. They'd actually think it was normal to get up at 6:00 on a Saturday morning and stand outside a house in the rain, waiting to be given a number so we could go in and pay money for someone's trash that will end up at our garage sale two years later. I'll bet I could even get them to wear tee shirts they can't trip over. They'd probably think it was cool.

In fact, if we lived in a solo-synchronized world, the concept of "cool" wouldn't even exist. I'll bet that raising an adolescent wouldn't be much more complicated than raising a goldfish if they weren't all trying to stay in sync with their friends. Of course, that's when parenting becomes a challenge. So we have to become realistic. To say, for example, that your daughter cannot go out with boys until she's old enough to receive birthday greetings from the White House would, simply, test her creativity. Rather than preventing her from dating, you would very likely help her begin to develop a complex system of subterfuge. She might say she's spending Friday night at her friend's house, but could be picking up truck drivers at the 7-11 for all you know.

Face it, our only chance is to try to build mutual trust and respect. Thus, rules need to seem fair to both parents and child. However, fairness does not, necessarily, mean agreement. As parents, it is not only our right to make the final decisions in these matters, but our responsibility. Fairness means sitting down together to discuss rules, listening to each other's views, and, finally, clarifying rules, privileges, and consequences. Agreeing on these rules would be like discovering that the act of chewing burns 100 calories a minute—something you'd read about in the *National Enquirer*.

So, when your daughter shrieks at you, "times have changed since you were my age, you know!" you can agree with her. While times have changed, the need for parents to draw the line has not. Since times have changed, you won't insist that she go to the movies on the back of a brontosaurus, but wherever you decide to draw the line you need to stick to it. Perhaps you'll agree that it's okay to go out in groups with boys and girls, but it is fair and important for a parent to want to know ahead of time whom a child is going to be with.

Encourage communication, not secrecy. However, to experience the peace of mind you deserve, I would highly recommend that you invest $4.79 in a goldfish with all the trimmings. Then, you can marvel as it surfaces to retrieve its daily grain of food: solo synchronized swimming at its world-class best.

Beyond Academics:
Expanding the Repertoire

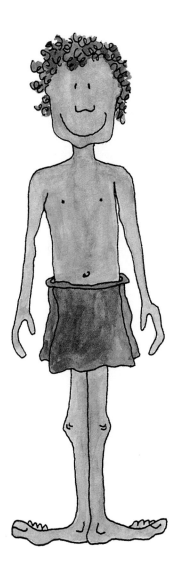

With the spring sports season fully upon us, I have decided to send you my nutritious meals-at-the-wheel recipes. These quick and easy recipes can all be prepared, served, AND EATEN while driving at a hair-raising 65 mph from the school to the orthodontist to the ball field to home to the ball field. "Pop-up pizza" and "gnats on a hard roll" do not even require utensils, an important time-saver. "Fast ball grinders" (meatball) can conveniently be used for pitching warm-ups in the back seat if you're running a bit late. However, I don't want to divulge all my culinary secrets. Besides, as seasoned sports parents, we have all succumbed to far greater indignities than merely eating "solar tuna" (tuna that, traditionally, should have been consumed by the bottom of the second, but is innovatively left to ripen on the front seat of the car and not retrieved until extra innings begin).

Yes, right now we are experiencing a more pervasive torment: the total disruption of family life as we once knew it. Having battled against telemarketing to maintain the uninterrupted family dinner, we now smile and call it "togetherness" when we can eat smushed peanut butter and jelly standing next to our six year old who is sharing his with the golden retriever who belongs to the other team's left fielder, as we proudly watch our kid shout "got it!" before completely missing the ball. Homework, too, seems to be a thing of the past. The routines that we all firmly adhered to in mid-winter are now overturned by practices, scrimmages, sliding clinics, and games.

The umpire's familiar "play ball" adds tension and stress to our fragmented lives. We know we're completely losing perspective when, feigning concern, we are deliriously THRILLED as Tom's mother tells us Tom vomited his high protein lunch all over the first three rows on the bus ride home and won't be able to pitch against our son's team that evening. We know we have truly gone over the edge when we want to stick out our tongues at the parents who actually flourish from all this wholesome activity. You know them. They bring the entire family, a picnic cooler, and even moist towelettes to every game. While my kids argue and compare goose bumps and blue lips in the shorts they insisted on wearing because the calendar said "Spring arrives today," these parents all smile, snugly wrapped up in the woolen blankets prudently stored in the back of the van for just such an occasion.

How do we regain a balanced perspective? We all signed our kids up and even agreed to help coach with the best of intentions. We wanted our kids to experience the thrill of being part of a team, the sense of camaraderie, the chance to build self-confidence, and perhaps, lastly, the opportunity to improve their ball skills. Maybe we need to forget about featuring each of the four food groups at dinner for a while. Maybe we can't expect ourselves to be at every, single game. Maybe sports are an opportunity for our child to demonstrate that he/she can finally assume responsibility for completing homework.

Maybe this season I'll be the mother smug and warm in the L.L. Bean blanket on the sidelines. Maybe I'll even tell you that the secret to my "Chips Marinara" is to marinate them from batting practice to the top of the sixth in spilled Gatorade. And, maybe I'll be the one who is crossing her fingers, secretly hoping we don't make it to the play-off games.

. . . .

"O-O-O-O-O-klahoma!" I boldly belted out, arms outstretched, standing on the dining room chair. What richness, what passion, what energy I possessed! Every nuance of the music was etched in my brain and burst from my fourteen year old heart. With tryouts less than one week away, I knew I could do it. I had even practiced lassoing the pet poodle in anticipation of the upcoming school musical.

This "Can Do" attitude enables us to take risks, make choices, and learn to trust our ability to make decisions. So, how do we help kids overcome the fear of failure, try out for the soccer team, the geography bee, or run for class president?

First, praise your child for having the courage to try, but it's best to avoid the "I just KNOW you'll make it" trap because, face it, you don't know. And, if he/she says that "Yangtze" is a Chinese baseball team and doesn't make the geography bee, as sure as "Lima" is more than a bean, it will be all YOUR fault—"I told you I couldn't do it, and you said I could. See, you don't know anything!" Instead, let your child know he/she has a really good chance of making the team. You could even offer to help review state capitals.

Next, let your kid know that he/she has your love and support no matter what the outcome. As a parent, I surely would rather have my kid experience kicking the winning soccer goal for the opponents with me around for comfort. It's safe to fail when you know you are loved for who you are and not what you accomplish.

Lastly, sometimes we work so hard to protect our children from failures and disappointments, we make "failure" seem like a criminal act punishable by banishment, twenty years hard labor, and an indelible stamp on the permanent record. In reality, it is the fear of failure that puts limits on our life. I remember when my son Brian was afraid to try out for the school baseball team. When I asked him why he was afraid, he wailed, "I might not make it." "Well," I shrieked with sensitivity, "you know who definitely won't make it? Billy Thompson, Jeffrey Rosenberg, Jamie DeSantis, and the ninety-eight other turkeys in your class who won't even try out! That's who won't make it!" Such understanding and compassion profoundly touched my son. He tried out, did not make it, and learned an important lesson.

In fact, we often learn more from our failures than our successes. Brian learned that he felt terrible for a day, but it wasn't terminal. And at fourteen, I learned how much confidence it takes to risk failing. Quite amazingly, on the afternoon of the *Oklahoma* auditions, an exotic strain of laryngitis happened to reach out and attack when my turn to audition arrived. So, I learned that there's something much worse than failing—not even trying.

. . . .

It was over ten years ago, but from the moment we secretly confessed to each other that our four years olds pushed Sarah Rosenberg off her "sit upon," it was instant friendship. While mothers obsessed over whether the nursery school curriculum was sufficiently challenging, I was fixated on whether Brian would ever expand his coloring repertoire beyond black. Thoroughly convinced I was the only nursery school mother whose child did not take Suzuki violin lessons, water aerobics, or subscribe to the *Wall Street Journal*, I was greatly relieved to find another humiliated mother who was cruelly aware she was raising a non-perfect child.

Without the mutual comfort and laughs, we might each have been certain we were rearing future subversives who would hijack senior citizens' busses, refuse to use utensils, and wear nothing but a loincloth even to Aunt Pearl's for Thanksgiving dinner. So, as our kids smeared peanut butter in each other's hair, we drank coffee and talked. We reassured each other about when to panic and when not to.

Ironically, now when we need this network of support more than ever, we operate in total isolation. We no longer get together for play groups. So, when our kids threaten to pierce their eyebrows, we never do find out that Vera's kid changed her mind the night Vera, Harry, and even Bozo the daschund sat down to dinner wearing clip-on gold hoops in their left eyebrow. As they ate their Spaghettios, nobody said a word and Vera's kid never mentioned piercing anything ever again.

Unfortunately, we are too immersed in our routines to take the time for collaboration. Funny, I can't decide which pair of pants to buy without consulting my friend. Yet, when our kids will talk to us only in monosyllabic grunts and we want to jump onto the kitchen table shrieking "YOU WERE SWITCHED AT BIRTH!," we talk to no one. Do not despair. Little League season provides the perfect opportunity to compare notes with other silently desperate parents. The hours we spend in the stands complaining about how the coach's kid always gets to play first base could be better spent breaking down the parent barrier. While we probably won't find solutions, it's still nice to know that our kid isn't the only one whose communication skills rival those of a male orangutan.

. . . .

I certainly never would have expected that selecting a birthday card for my daughter, Tam, would make me want to picket Hallmark, Inc., but as I read through the "Happy Birthday, Daughter" selections, I learned that some daughters are "pretty and some are smart, and some are funny"…but "you, Daughter, are PERFECT." Ah, come on! "Perfect" describes a one hundred on a spelling test or a double fudge chocolate cake, not a human being. I want my daughter to see herself as the unique, zany person she is: a wonderful combination of inconsistencies and contradictions, not a Barbie doll. And, of course, this artificial standard isn't even attainable. So, we're setting up our daughters for failure.

Although we have made progress in minimizing gender stereotyping, we continue to perpetuate it with messages from the media. Actually, do you realize that card browsing is a great way to discover what matters to us? Women, it would seem, are obsessed with three things: their thighs, their age, and how much more attractive their friends are. Men, evidently, are presented as thinking only of sex, drinking, and sports.

Thus, gender stereotyping shortchanges males as well as females. If boys are not interested in greeting their friends by putting them in a head lock and giving them a noogie, they might be considered a bit weird. If they'd rather play the piano than slop around in the mud trying to catch a football, they feel embarrassed about it. So how do you help your son feel good about who he is when he doesn't want to eat road kill and spit tobacco?

- Show an active interest in his activities. Parents have frequently been caught sneaking out of work early just to freeze on the soccer sidelines. You wouldn't even have to jeopardize your career in order to be involved in his music lessons. Why not listen to him practice Beethoven with the same interest with which you would watch the soccer scrimmage? Shouting an occasional, "sounds good" from the garage with the belt sander going is not quite the same as sitting in the living room for ten minutes with him.

- Ask questions about his music. What is the hardest (favorite, easiest, etc.) piece he's working on? What makes that piece difficult? What went well at the lesson:? How are you going to get that scale up to tempo? Come on, it's got to beat entire dinner conversations centered around how the halfback from Cheshire blocked the corner kick and wasn't even wearing a cup!

The media may try to tell us what to be like, but we certainly don't all have to fall for it. Take my cousin Irma, for example. When she read the ad, "I lost 39 pounds and found a husband," she blurted out, "that's the best advertisement for fat I ever saw!"

. . . .

Esther's mother Ida died six days ago and I will miss the chocolate eclairs she always brought from Schwartz's Bakery out on the island. You may know the kind—the vanilla custard oozing out from one end when you take the first bite and the chocolate icing ending up on the tip of your nose so that you strut around with it all day thinking, "God, I must look TERRIFIC in that new black skirt!" cause everyone is smiling at you at work.

She always remembered to bring an extra one for me.

I went to pay a condolence call the other night. Esther's very closest friends were all there to comfort her and as I waited for my turn to express my sadness, I couldn't help but overhear the woman in front of me say, brimming with emotion, "Esther, I'm so-o-o-o- upset! Do you think I REALLY look as old as Ruthie?" Obviously, some of us are more adept at these awkward, painful moments than others, I thought, restraining myself from lunging across the chopped liver platter and gagging her with an onion bagel.

As adults, most of us don't know how to help a grieving friend, so how can we begin to advise our kids about helping their friends who are experiencing grief? Here are a few suggestions:

- Help them formulate a brief statement such as, "I'm so sorry about your _____ (grandma, grandpa, etc.)." There's no need to say any more even though we usually feel the need to fill a silence.
- Encourage your child to call and invite the friend to come over. Kids always welcome an escape from Aunt Pearl who has been pinching their cheeks and telling them how much they've grown since she saw them last with diapers and, at the same time, stuffing salami sandwiches and marble cheesecake into her pocketbook for the ride home.
- In the weeks and months that follow, suggest that your child ask, "How are you doing?" every now and then. It is tempting to want friends to quickly put their grief behind them, but that isn't realistic. We must grieve and recover at our own pace and, chances are, it will be a slower and more difficult struggle than we could imagine. So, tell your child not to be afraid to keep inquiring. It lets a friend know you care.

After a brief period normal life resumes, but for those closely touched by the grief, getting back to normal won't even be possible again. "Normal" has changed forever because Esther's mother Ida died six days ago and I will miss the chocolate eclairs she brought from Schwartz's Bakery and because she always remembered to bring an extra one for me.

Togetherness:
Devil's Island Revisited

Wasn't this the year that you were going to be finished with your holiday shopping by Thanksgiving, address and mail your cards by December 1st, bake and freeze by last July 4th? Ah, the joys of the holiday season are upon us before we even can shake our fist and snarl, "that's MY parking place. I got here first!" There's the tingle of excitement as we pray that our check won't bounce, the heart-warming sight of humanity stretching from the checkout line to the Twinkies aisle, the hardened lumps of cookie dough permanently stuck to the kitchen counter, the five pounds of cookie dough permanently stuck to our hips. This joyous season brings the spirit of upward mobility to us all.

Pressures of time and commitments are not new to our generation. Even Robert Frost understood mall-o-mania:

"The woods are lovely, dark, and deep,

But I have promises to keep,

And miles to go before I sleep."

A year ago I received this anonymous note from a student. "For the past few years our family has never had great holidays and this year everybody refuses to be happy. Everything they say is negative. They are missing the real reason for this season and it upsets me."

Maybe, especially during the stressful holidays, as parents we need to ask for help doing the dishes, fixing the salad, walking the dog, so we can still have time and energy to help with homework and, simply, listen to our kids. Rather than pretending to do it all, we need to enlist their support and understanding. Kids need to feel needed. Give them an opportunity to give of themselves. Years from now they will remember the game of Charades you played together more than the Nintendo game you raced out to buy.

. . . .

SURPRISE ME! That's the gift I really want from my family this year. As sure as kids would walk around wearing flocked wallpaper if all their friends did it, we women can count on getting a bottle of "Eau de Manure" that is sure to make us turn green and pass out on the first spritz as we try not to inhale. Wouldn't it be a refreshing change to experience a surprise, instead? So, here's my list:

- turn down my bed at night and leave a single red rose on my pillow.
- make my lunch.
- let me wear your clothes and put them back dirty.
- write me a poem wrapped in a green floral package.
- take me to a psychic.
- give me Kevin Costner's home address.
- leave a message on the refrigerator saying, "I'll cook tonight. You go up and take a bubble bath."
- tuck me in.
- get Jane Fonda's thighs to jiggle.
- read to me.
- give me dental floss coated in Godiva chocolate.
- send me funny cards at work.

Only one day after I had strategically stuck copies of this list on the remote control, the telephone receiver, the toilet paper dispenser, and the bag of Halloween candy hidden above the dryer under piles of unmatched socks, my wish had been granted. Faith had been restored as I held in my hand a sealed envelope with "MOM—PRIVATE" neatly scripted on the front. Wishing to savor the moment, I felt inspired to skip upstairs and leave a peppermint patty on everyone's pillow. I wanted to heat their bath towels in the microwave, I couldn't wait to…The true spirit of giving was infectious. In the midst of this euphoria, I greedily tore open the envelope:

"Sorry, Mom. I'll bet you never thought I could do this badly on a history test! All the kids in the class got bad grades—most were even worse than mine. I really need you to sign this so I can return it to Mr. Turnbull by tomorrow. Love, Guess who?"

I have to give him credit. I was surprised.

. . . .

Togetherness: that's what snow days are all about. It's time to bring out the old Monopoly game, the 10,000 piece jigsaw puzzle, and Grandma's chocolate chip cookie recipe. Everyone can sit around together and watch *The Wizard of Oz* for the thirty-seventh time. Time to teach the kids to play chess. Time to make Valentines for each other. Time to finish putting the photos into albums. Right? WRONG!

After being blitzed by, yet, another Siberian tornado, I feel as if I'm part of a forced labor camp charged with shoveling out the gulag. The human body and spirit are being pushed to the limits and there are sure signs that the mind appears to be losing the battle. Why, I have even begun to devise terrorist tactics to keep the street plow from blocking our driveway. I just ordered a "diamonique" ring and a battery-operated pepper grinder that I don't need from the home shopping channel, and when my mother called from Elsie's place in Florida to tell me about her new putter, I growled back to her to send the putter to me so I could put it to good use chopping the ice off the roof.

Extraordinary times call for some extraordinary measures. It may mean locking yourself in the bathroom to read the classifieds upside-down to have some privacy or calling your best friend, the soul-mate who always has the ability to ground you. Shocking as it may be, your kids may have had enough togetherness as well. We all need to be creative about structuring some privacy for ourselves.

Take my friend, Nancy, for instance. As I ignored three call-waiting signals to get Nancy on the phone, I felt a calmness descending just from hearing her soothing voice on the other end. "Carol, excuse me for just a minute," she gently purred. With the roads navigable only by dogsled she shrieked to her daughter, "Sure, I'll drive you to Jennifer's house and don't come back till you have more liver spots than a springer spaniel!"

Nancy, thanks. I feel better already.

· · · · · · · · · ·

The dreaded annual holiday letter from Muffy Smith-Clark, a college friend, arrived yesterday. "The entire nuclear family will be vacationing in Geneva to be with my sister and her family who are currently residing in Monaco. And, would you believe, they have a simply MAHVELOUS view of the palace!!! We really need this break because it's been an ever so difficult fall for us all. We've had to travel all over the northeast with Brent Jr. who must decide by Febs whether to apply to Princeton early decision or try Dartmouth, Yale, and Amherst. Dear friends, the truth is, we're a bit concerned that his B in AP history last year could prove to be devastating to his permanent record. All this focus on Brent Jr. has not been easy for Marshall. He doesn't appreciate the fact that he's only a sophomore, and yet, he's the starting quarterback for the varsity team. Poor dear, he's still pouting about having come in second place in the declamation contest last May and is, now, convinced that he will end up in a state university!!! Can you imagine, really???" After a nauseating account of the "finger bowl fiasco" at Thanksgiving dinner, PS., PPS., P.P.P.S…, we have the final "P.P.P.P.P.S. Note the newest member of our family, 'Lolita,' our Afghan."

Well, Muffy, here's my letter to you. "Let me tell you about our Norman Rockwell Thanksgiving at my parents' house. After dinner, my nine year old nephew, Howard, decided the wishbone would be his and his alone and proceeded to take possession of it by ingesting it, much to my mother's horror. I, secretly, had made my own wish that he would do just that. And, would you believe, we returned to a spectacular view, too? The recent heavy rains flooded our basement, so Bill did an impressive 40 laps while I used the kids' flippers and snorkel to check out the floating paint cans hoping to rescue the Harvest Gold to touch up the bathroom."

Why is it that receiving these letters makes me feel as if I live in a cardboard box in Grand Central Station and my kids are no-necked monsters who will still be mimicking each other long after their teeth are in jars at night? Maybe I should tell Muffy about my daughter waking me up to surprise me with tea and burnt toast when I was sick last week. Maybe Muffy would like to hear about my son's recycling all the litter he found on his way home from school today. Or, that I was finally on the winning Pictionary team last night after dinner. Maybe she'd be excited to hear about the fortune cookies we made for each other or that Brian folded everyone's laundry or that Tam left notes on everyone's pillow or that…Actually, I don't think so. My life just doesn't look impressive on paper.

As I squint and extend my arm to check out Muffy's family photo, I give up. The entire nuclear family looks like they just won "Best in Breed" at Westminster. So come on, which one is Lolita? Aha! There she is: the one on the right with the tongue hanging down.

Letting Go:
Not Until Their Teeth are in a Jar

"Ethel, I tell you, he absolutely refuses to go and threatens to run away from camp if I make him go!" I knew I could count on Ethel, the summer camp guru, to give me good advice.

"Look", she counseled, "last year I sent Martin to camp and insisted he leave all the tags on his new camp gear until he was sure he was staying. It worked."

"It worked?"

"It worked."

Ten blissful weeks of summer vacation! Ten blissful weeks of beach sand embedded in your family room rug, mildewed towels wadded up on the back seat of the car, and seedless green grape fights. Ten blissful weeks of "but, Mom, there's nothing to do around here." What better motivation is needed for a parent to feverishly pursue summer camp information? It is never too early to begin. In fact, it might already be too late since other parents, you know, the ones who would never serve peanut butter and jelly for dinner, have probably reserved the few remaining spaces at Camp Wa-cha-wanna-do. While kids certainly need a break from the pace and structure of the school year, they still seem to thrive on constant activity. Unless you are prepared to wear a whistle, a tee shirt that says, "My name is Stinky. Return to Bunk 6," and play, "human amoeba," you might want to consider the possibility of some planned summer programs. Here are just a few pointers.

- Ignore all pleas of "I don't want to go to camp. I'll have lots to do." Remember that this is the same kid who is bored between walking in the door and sticking a head in the refrigerator, complaining that there's nothing to eat around here.

- Provide alternatives for your child. You could say, "Dear, it's up to you. Would you prefer to go to Camp Neeto for two weeks or spend those two weeks at home doing a twenty page research paper on Europe's feudal order, scrubbing the toilets, building your vocabulary, and sitting with your mother at the beach?"

- Be reasonable. If your child has never gone away to camp before, it might not be wise to insist that he/she spend an entire eight weeks as a Tuscarora at Camp Koo-chee-koo in Bangor, Maine. However, if you choose a more local camp, I would strongly advise you to do what Ethel did with Martin. She threw him into the car, left two days early, and drove to camp by way of Nebraska. Martin never knew.
- Finally, be supportive. When your kids threaten to run away from camp if you make them go, Ethel, it turns out, had a practical solution. Never one to throw good money away, she knew what she was doing. But, for the first two weeks, Martin was stuck being Peewee Malloy's water buddy cause he was always late for swimming, shuffling to the lake with his brand new flip-flops still tagged together.

· · · · · · · · · ·

"What do you think of this dress, Mom?" Vulgar was the first word that came to mind: six inches above the knee, everything-less (sleeveless, backless, scooped neck), and so tight that it could only be pried from her body with a putty knife. "Why, it's lovely, dear, but I don't think chartreuse is really your color."

Shopping for the eighth grade graduation dress seems to represent a rite of passage between parent and daughter. It is in the fitting room that the struggle for identity and independence is played out. The way in which we handle these interactions is like the way earthquake victims react. Some panic and try to hold up the walls; others open the freezer, grab a pint of Ben and Jerry's Super Fudge Chunk, and wait it out in the basement. When it comes to clothing, I've been quite proud of my "wait it out in the basement" attitude. I've gagged discreetly behind my daughter's back as the paisley leggings stuck out from under her father's boxers on her way to the bus. However, this particular occasion was more difficult for me.

There was no in between. Some of the dresses we saw looked like grossly larger versions of the dresses we foisted upon our daughters for their second birthday party right before they sat on the cake. Other dresses would have looked much more appropriate on the set of *Melrose Place*. Although our daughters seem to be caught between two worlds, they certainly don't seem to want their mothers deciding which one they fit into.

Stories of fitting room battles have been known to reach Biblical proportions. Take the story of Margie and her daughter Lisa. Lisa fell in love with the dress that had feathers around the bodice, while Margie loved the floral taffeta, mid-calf, bell sleeved dress. The battle began as a polite stand-off, escalated to shouts of "I refuse to look like the living room drapes," and continued in front of the 3-way mirror. Margie shrieked to everyone in the store, even the men snoring on the bench next to the sales rack, "Would you let YOUR daughter wear a dress that looked like furry lingerie?" Margie refused to pay for it. Lisa said she'd pay for it herself. They pulled and tugged and pretty soon feathers were flying and, with Solomon-like precision, the dress ripped right down its twenty inch length.

The fitting room relationship is truly the measure of a mother/daughter relationship. So we need to deal with it in a manner consistent with our beliefs, standards, and priorities. How do we balance giving our children the freedom to make their own mistakes with the reality check they need? Sticking to the facts and avoiding emotionally charged statements can help. Remember, your opinion matters more than they will ever let you know. I did let my daughter know that I thought the dress was too tight, but before the discussion became adversarial, we put the dress on "hold" for an hour, looked around the mall, and sat down with a frozen strawberry yogurt and pretzel with mustard. There we were, giggling about the five year old nearby helping himself to Reese's Pieces topping as his mother waited for her change. When we were ready to return to the dress, I was confident that we would both be reasonable.

But, why doesn't she have the sense to wear a sweater? I'm freezing!

. . . .

Eighth grade graduation is that time when, discreetly carrying the video camera, tripod, four roles of 35 mm film, a telephoto lens, and special laser flash attachment, you inflict the final humiliation upon your child: you attempt to pose your child in such a way to imply that this entire ceremony is solely in his/her honor. Armed with more photographic equipment than was used to shoot *Jurassic Park,* you outsmart the 219 other parents and hang by your toes from the second floor bathroom window for the perfect vantage point. However, middle school graduation is not a moment in time to be captured in a snapshot. Rather, it is a time of discovery.

Self-discovery is a lifelong process (except in the case of my Aunt Selma whom

Uncle Bernie said was so sweet. "I don't know what happened to her," he said, befuddled. "She turned fifteen, fell down the elevator shaft, landed on her head," and was inexplicably, plunged into a sort of permanent adolescence). This time of discovery seems to be stuck on fast-forward at this point in your children's life. They really need to expand their notion of who they are and where they fit into their new community.

As high school freshmen, your children will have opportunities to participate in musical groups, social action groups, sports, theater, art, politics, etc. regardless of their level of competence. While keeping up with the academics is important, my two resident experts (both high school juniors) emphatically agreed that the students who do not get involved in extracurricular activities seem to be the ones who get into more trouble.

As parents, then, how do you get them to identify with the spring musical instead of the stink bomb brigade? If they need you to insist that they choose one activity, then, go ahead. But, when you imagined your kid being carried off the field by his team after scoring the winning touchdown in the big game and he decides to go out for the debate team instead, you need to be there to cheer just as loudly. You need to help out with rides when you can and help make the activities accessible. "Letting go" doesn't mean letting alone. It means we must be involved, but in a new way. We must guide, but not control. We must support, but not stifle.

As sure as you'll forget to remove the lens cap from the video camera, your eighth graders will step forth together as a class. A challenge, as parents, is not to be trampled by them or to step out of their way, but be prepared to step forth along with them as they begin this meandering journey.

EPILOGUE
Change is More than Reupholstering the Couch

I knew something was wrong when I folded all the laundry, discovered that each sock neatly matched, and promptly burst into tears. For eighteen years the pile of unmatched socks above the washing machine had spread like some sort of slime threatening to turn us all green. Then, this fall Tam and Brian each went off to college and we have precision-matched socks now. Nobody prepared me for this.

I had done so well up to now. In fact, if Ethel is the summer camp guru, then surely, I am the letting-go guru. It isn't as if their leaving is a surprise. But, it's a little like going to your spouse's office Christmas party. Knowing it will be worse than going to a Three Stooges film festival doesn't make it any easier when the time comes. A month ago, the thought that it would be just Bill and me would have been wonderful, but now it sent me catapulting out the front door to my next door neighbor. We sipped an herbal infusion and listened to James Taylor tapes and I felt calmer—until the next day when I went grocery shopping. I had always hated wheeling the shopping cart mindlessly up and down the aisles, so I would make up little games, you know, like pretending to be Martha Stewart shopping for her upcoming White House luncheon. I'd color coordinate all the items in the cart: red on the bottom, moving up to green, then on to violet. Just picture the tomatoes, if you can, by the time they got to the check-out line. Anyhow, this time I sobbed past the hamburger helper and was close to hysteria by the time I reached the deli counter. I had no reason to get any of these things. I left with some peach yogurt, a bottle of cleanser, and my 50¢ off Sugar Smacks coupon.

Poor Bill was helpless at helping me through this period. I was grieving and just needed to recover on my own time-table. I wallowed in self-pity, said Kaddish over car-pooling, and hated that I could see what color the carpeting in their bedrooms was once again. But I learned that the best way to cope was to move forward in my own life. Change and growth not only enrich our life, but the lives of those closest to us.

Changing and letting go enable us to grow along with our children rather than be left behind like the Cabbage Patch kid in their closets.

So, I started by reupholstering the living room couch and moved on from there. Last week I even became a high-tech mom and e-mailed Tam with an urgent message: "Help! How do I get Grandma to stop calling me so often?" Without hesitation, she replied, "Why don't you just tell her? You can say, 'it was great talking to you, Mom. I've got a really busy week coming up so I'll call you over the weekend.'" She was right. It worked. Yesterday, I had even resorted to squeezing my nose and pretending to be the answering machine when I heard my mother's voice and she left a ten minute message anyway. How gratifying to be able to turn to my daughter for advice! As we each evolve so does the relationship. Obviously, there are many ways in which she has surpassed me.

What greater reward is there for parents, than to have their children go beyond them as individuals? My children and I are exploring a new phase. We'll make many mistakes and we will learn from each other as we always have. Throughout the years I nurtured their infancy, I cherished their childhood, and I celebrated their adolescence. Now, I'm reveling in their adulthood. Do I have any regrets when I look back? It is the things we don't do that we regret—not the things we do. I have no regrets.